D1374078

Can You Find These Birds?

Carmen Bredeson and Lindsey Cousins

Enslow Elementary

an imprint of

Enslow Publishers, Inc.

40 Industrial Road
Box 398
Berkeley Heights, NJ 07922
USA

http://www.enslow.com

Enslow Elementary, an imprint of Enslow Publishers, Inc.
Enslow Elementary® is a registered trademark of Enslow Publishers, Inc.

Library of Congress Cataloging-in-Publication Data

Bredeson, Carmen.
  Can you find these birds? / Carmen Bredeson and Lindsey Cousins.
    p. cm. — (All about nature)
  Includes index.
  Summary: "Learn about different birds including robins, woodpeckers, and mockingbirds"—Provided
by publisher.
  ISBN 978-0-7660-3977-3
  1. Birds—Juvenile literature. 2. Birds—Identification—Juvenile literature. I. Cousins, Lindsey. II.
Title.
  QL676.2.B723 2012598—dc23
                                        2011026420

Future editions:
Paperback ISBN 978-1-4644-0072-8
ePUB ISBN 978-1-4645-0979-7
PDF ISBN 978-1-4646-0979-4

Printed in China
012012 Leo Paper Group, Heshan City, Guangdong, China
10 9 8 7 6 5 4 3 2 1

Note to Parents and Teachers

Help pre-readers get a jump start on reading. These lively stories introduce simple concepts with
repetition of words and short simple sentences. Photos and illustrations fill the pages with color and
effectively enhance the text. Free Educator Guides are available for this series at www.enslow.com.
Search for the *All About Nature* series name.

Contents

Words to Know

beak (beek)

female (FEE mayl)

male (mayl)

Birds

Birds sit on fences.

Birds sing in the trees.

Birds hop along the ground.

Birds are all around us.

Birds are many colors.

Go outside and look around.

Can you find some of the birds

in this book?

Males have a red spot on the back of their heads.

Downy Woodpecker

These birds are black and white.

They make a lot of noise.

They drum their *beaks* on wood.

Rat-a-tat! Rat-a-tat!

This noise is their song.

Crow

Crows are black.

They make loud caw-caw sounds.

Crows eat worms and bugs.

They eat fruit and garbage too.

Crows eat a lot of things.

Robin

Robins hop around the grass.

They look for worms.

Robins lay blue eggs.

Baby robins hatch from the eggs.

House sparrows are brown and gray. Males have a black spot under their beak. It looks like a bib!

House Sparrow

Look in your yard.

You may see a sparrow.

These little birds are everywhere.

They peck at the ground.

Sparrows eat seeds and bugs.

Pigeon

Pigeons do not hop like other birds.

They walk.

Their heads bob up and down.

Pigeons make coo-coo-coo sounds.

They are fun to feed in the park.

male

female

Goldfinch

The *male* bird is bright yellow.

It has a black spot on its head.

The *female* is yellow and brown.

Fill your bird feeder with seeds.

Goldfinches may visit you.

They eat seeds from flowers too.

Barn Swallow

These birds zip through the air.

They catch bugs while they fly.

Barn swallows have long tails.

Their tails look like the letter V.

female

male

Cardinal

Look for a bright red bird.

It may be a male cardinal.

Female cardinals are

mostly brown.

But they both have red beaks.

Cardinals are also called redbirds.

Mockingbird

Mockingbirds are loud.

They copy other bird sounds.

They even copy bug sounds.

Sometimes mockingbirds

sing all night.

Chirp! Chirp! Chirp!

Read More

Hudak, Heather. *Robins: World of Wonder Watch Them Grow.* New York: Weigl Publishers Inc., 2011.

Sill, Cathryn. *About Birds: A Guide For Children.* Atlanta: Peachtree Publishers, 1997.

Williams, Brenda. *Amazing Birds.* Pleasantville, N.Y.: Gareth Stevens Publishing, 2008.

Web Sites

Enchanted Learning. *All About Birds.* <http://www.enchantedlearning.com/subjects/birds/>

San Diego Zoo Kids. *Birds.* <http://kids.sandiegozoo.org/animals/birds>

Index

Guided Reading Level: E
Guided Reading Leveling System is based on the guidelines recommended by Fountas and Pinnell.

Word Count: 274